IMAGES
of America

BRYAN

This postcard, postmarked 1909, shows the Williams County Courthouse in Bryan, Ohio. (Photograph by John Beach; courtesy of the Williams County Public Library Local History Center.)

ON THE COVER: This postcard shows a carnival in Bryan on July 4, 1908. (Photograph by John Beach; courtesy of the Williams County Public Library Local History Center.)

IMAGES
of America

BRYAN

Walter E. Grunden

ARCADIA
PUBLISHING

Published by Arcadia Publishing
Charleston, South Carolina

Library of Congress Control Number: 2012953502

For all general information, please contact Arcadia Publishing:
Telephone 843-853-2070
Fax 843-853-0044
E-mail sales@arcadiapublishing.com
For customer service and orders:
Toll-Free 1-888-313-2665

Visit us on the Internet at www.arcadiapublishing.com

In loving memory of Hannah M. (Schlosser)
Allomong Hulbert (1900–1970).

CONTENTS

ACKNOWLEDGMENTS

This book could not have been written without the assistance and cooperation of Jane Kelly, Joyce Yoder, and the staff at the Williams County Public Library Local History Center. Thank you for all your help. My stalwart and trusty student intern, Rebecca Pawlowicz, also deserves a lot of credit for scanning the photographs and being an otherwise resourceful assistant. I am also indebted to Kara Custar, executive director of the Williams County Historical Society in Montpelier, Ohio, for assistance in acquiring and identifying additional photographs. Eldon and Marlene Smith kindly shared an afternoon going through an early draft of the manuscript with me and helped to fill in numerous gaps. I also could not have made my way through the captions as quickly or efficiently without relying on the work already done by Kevin Maynard, who was at this long before I came along. I would also like to thank the staff of the Bowling Green State University Center for Archival Collections, especially Lee McLaird, for assistance in accessing sources in this collection. There are so many photographers who deserve credit that it is difficult to name them all. Among those whose works are prominently featured here are John Beach, C.C. Garber, Robert Lindsey, Paul van Gundy, Carla Allshouse, and Eldon Smith. This book simply would not exist but for them. I would also like to thank my parents, Elwood Grunden, and Dale and Marilyn Taylor, because most of what I know about Bryan comes from having lived under their roof. Special recognition also goes to my colleague and long-time friend, Professor Clark Hultquist, who inspired and encouraged me to take on this project after completing his own book for Arcadia Publishing. My editor, Sandy Shalton, was ever so patient, and I owe her both apologies and gratitude for indulging me with extended deadlines and revisions. Finally, I wish to thank my wife and best friend, Han Li, who must be the most patient and supportive person I have ever known. Unless otherwise indicated, all photographs were provided courtesy of the Williams County Public Library Local History Center.

INTRODUCTION

It is difficult to imagine a time when there were trees as far as the eye could see and no passable roads to ease the journey across the land when looking at downtown Bryan today. Just 200 years ago, most of northwest Ohio looked much the same as it had for thousands of years. The terrain was inhospitable—a humid marsh full of mosquitoes in the summer and a frozen wilderness in the winter. The indigenous peoples—Miami, Pottawatomie, and Wyandotte—survived on abundant fish and wild game. The many rivers, creeks, ponds, and lakes in the area teemed with pike, bass, crappie, bluegill, perch, and trout. Deer and wild turkey were everywhere. The equally ever-present fox, otter, beaver, and raccoon were less desirable as food but provided pelts for clothing and later for trade. Black bear, wolves, bobcats, and panthers freely roamed the land but did not threaten the existence of the Indian.

But the Battle of Fallen Timbers near present-day Maumee in 1794 brought about the demise of the Western Confederacy of American Indian tribes and resulted in the signing of the Treaty of Greenville the following year. The treaty opened the Northwest Territory to settlement, and ceded much of the land that is today Ohio to the nascent government of the United States. In time, intrepid pioneers forged their way west and established forts and villages that grew into cities, such as Cincinnati (founded in 1788), Cleveland (1796), and Columbus (1812). Ohio was the first state to be carved out of the Northwest Territory and was admitted to the Union in 1803. Columbus became its capital in 1816.

Not long after, surveyors began to plot the lands of northwest Ohio and several counties were designated, including Wood (1820), Henry (1820), and Williams County (1824). Nevertheless, development came more slowly to the northwest region of the state. Toledo, founded in 1833 as part of the Michigan Territory, was beginning to prosper as a trade hub due to its strategic location at the mouth of the Maumee River on Lake Erie. But the "Great Black Swamp," a vast marshland stretching from the western shores of Lake Erie to the eastern border of Indiana, remained a formidable barrier to travel and development. Only the rivers made the area reasonably accessible.

Because of its location at the confluence of the Maumee and Auglaize Rivers, Defiance emerged as one of the first major settlements in northwest Ohio. Founded as Fort Defiance in 1794 by Gen. "Mad" Anthony Wayne, a village grew steadily around the fort as the rivers brought commerce, pioneers, and developers. When Williams County was established in 1824, it was Defiance that was designated as the first county seat. In 1825, two state representatives signed a contract with the founders of Defiance, pledging that it would remain so "permanently." But within a mere decade, there were already calls for a change. In the 1830s, new counties were formed, and the boundaries of existing ones were altered. When the present borders of Putnam and Henry Counties were determined in 1834, and those of Paulding County five years later, the changes removed land from Williams County and left Defiance in the southeast corner, far from the center as it once was. The changes did not meet the approval of the growing populace of northern Williams County.

Meanwhile, developers were busy buying up the land. John Alexander Bryan and his partner, Dr. William Trevitt, bought, surveyed, and plotted much of Williams County for the American Land Company of New York. Both were also politically connected. Bryan was recently elected state auditor, and Trevitt was elected to the state legislature in 1836 to represent Perry County. Whether it was by actual popular demand or by Bryan and Trevitt's political maneuvering, by 1839, a groundswell of support emerged for moving the county seat. The state legislature resolved in the spring of 1839 to let the people of Williams County decide the issue by popular vote, and the resolution passed in the autumn of that year by a large majority. The search for a new county seat began. Several villages were in contention, but Bryan already had the very place in mind.

On July 1, 1840, the county locating committee in Columbus accepted an offer from Bryan and Trevitt to relocate the county seat from Defiance to the southwest quarter of Section 17 of Pulaski Township. According to local historians Richard Cooley and Kevin Maynard, Bryan and Trevitt pledged to provide "two acres in the center of the proposed town for a public square." To sweeten the deal, Bryan and Trevitt also promised to construct a "temporary" courthouse before the next spring and within four years would also construct "neat and appropriate public buildings" for no less than $8,500.

Two weeks later, on July 14, 1840, Miller Arrowsmith, the official surveyor of Williams County, finished charting the town plat in Pulaski Township at the center of Williams County, which the American Land Company owned. The plat was drawn with 182 lots and a town square, and legend has it that it was modeled after the state capital, Columbus, with the two central cross streets being named "Main" and "High." Arrowsmith inked the name of the new town he plotted—Bryan. Thus, a village was born.

Understandably, when the people of Defiance learned of the deal they were incensed, as were those who had lost the bid. As Cooley and Maynard wrote in *Temple of Justice: The Story of Williams County's Courthouses*, "The consensus of the losers was that money made the difference in the selection, and some believed the site was chosen before the committee left Columbus. Certainly some of them noticed one of the locating committee was from Dr. Trevitt's home county (Perry County)." Whether it was money or political influence that finally determined the outcome remains uncertain, but the deal was done. Bryan would be the new seat of Williams County.

In the summer of 1840, the village of Bryan existed only on paper. Within the lines drawn on the map, there were only dense forests of elm, beech, oak, ash, sugar maple, walnut, and linden trees, all growing out of standing pools of water. By all descriptions from the time, Bryan was nothing more than a swamp. But before long, founder John Bryan hired crews to clear the land and, by the end of the year, a temporary, two-story log courthouse stood at what is today the intersection of North Main and East Mulberry Streets. Trees were felled on two lots at the center of town making way for a more permanent courthouse and public square.

On February 22, 1841, Bryan bought from the American Land Company some 960 acres in the heart of Williams County for himself, including the county seat bearing his name. He sold a half interest in the town parcel to Trevitt and, as promised, they deeded to the county two central lots for a town square. Two days later, on February 24, the move from Defiance to Bryan began. Settlers soon arrived. Daniel Wyatt is credited with having built the first house in Bryan—"a log cabin on the south side of the courthouse square." William Yates opened a dry goods store and became the village's first merchant. Daniel Langel built the Mansion House hotel near Yates's on the east side of the square. And, by 1846, a new, two-story brick courthouse graced the center of the village.

Bryan was officially incorporated as a village on March 7, 1849. The town grew slowly in that first decade, but in 1855, the Michigan Southern and Northern Indiana Railroad expanded its line west from Toledo through Bryan. The rail brought new economic opportunity. Farmers soon had a freight depot where they could load their grain for sale. Elevators and gristmills were built, and merchants arrived to meet the growing demand for daily necessities. More land was cleared for settlement. More families arrived. All the while, the Great Black Swamp was being drained from Toledo to Bryan. Ditches were dug, and corduroy and plank roads crisscrossed northwest Ohio.

Bryan's high water table, once a major impediment to development, was now a blessing. Those first settlers did not have to dig very far down to find clean water. Artesian wells could be bored just about anywhere and strike water at only 10 to 20 feet deep. The spring water was clear and cold, and many used backyard wells as a crude form of refrigeration. Bryan's reputation as a source of good water percolated throughout the region, soon earning the county seat the appellation "The Fountain City."

A growing population required improved infrastructure and services. By the 1860s, the old, wood-frame buildings surrounding the square were being replaced by solid brick structures such as the Union Block, the Letcher Block, and, later in 1876, the Centennial Block. A series of fires downtown in the 1870s, including one case of suspected arson by an overzealous temperance activist that destroyed most of the buildings on the south side of the square, coupled with a rare earthquake in 1884, left the environs of the square and the old courthouse in disrepair.

In 1888, the village elders of Bryan successfully lobbied the state legislature for funds to build a new courthouse. The old building was razed, and construction on the new began the next year. Designed by Toledo architect Edward O. Fallis, and built by the contracting firm of Malone Brothers and Earhart, the present-day Williams County Courthouse was completed in 1900 at a cost of approximately $250,000. According to courthouse historians Cooley and Maynard, "The building's architectural style is that of modified French Baroque, influenced by Romanesque Revival." When finished, the courthouse and the surrounding Court Park became the centerpiece of Williams County and the heart of the Bryan community.

Bryan continued to grow and prosper through the turn of the century. Merchant stores opened around the square, such as the Bryan Dry Goods Company, W.H. Moore's, Long's, Culbertson's, Garn's, and Hartman's drugstores. Two banks—the First National and Farmers National (later Citizens National)—provided the community's financial services. Although Williams County profited somewhat from northwest Ohio's brief oil and natural gas boom in the 1880s and 1890s, Wood, Henry, and Hancock Counties fared much better. Agriculture remained the mainstay of Bryan's economy well into the 20th century, until new immigrants and local entrepreneurs brought industrial development to the town.

Prosperity, community, and history have given the people of Bryan much to celebrate. For decades, Independence Day has been commemorated with parades, a carnival or jubilee, and, from 1976, a "Day in the Park," capped off with fireworks and a performance of the city band. The Court Park downtown and the city's many municipal parks, such as Moore and Garver Park, have provided verdant spaces for celebration. The bandstands in Court Park provided venues for Saturday and Wednesday night band performances in the summers, as well as a temporary shelter for Santa's workshop in December. A county fair has been held in late summer every year since 1856.

Bryan can also celebrate its people. In the course of its history, Bryan's sons and daughters have excelled in the arts and entertainment, higher education, business and finance, law, military service, medicine, science, and especially sports. What follows is only part of the story of the Fountain City—"a great place to live!"

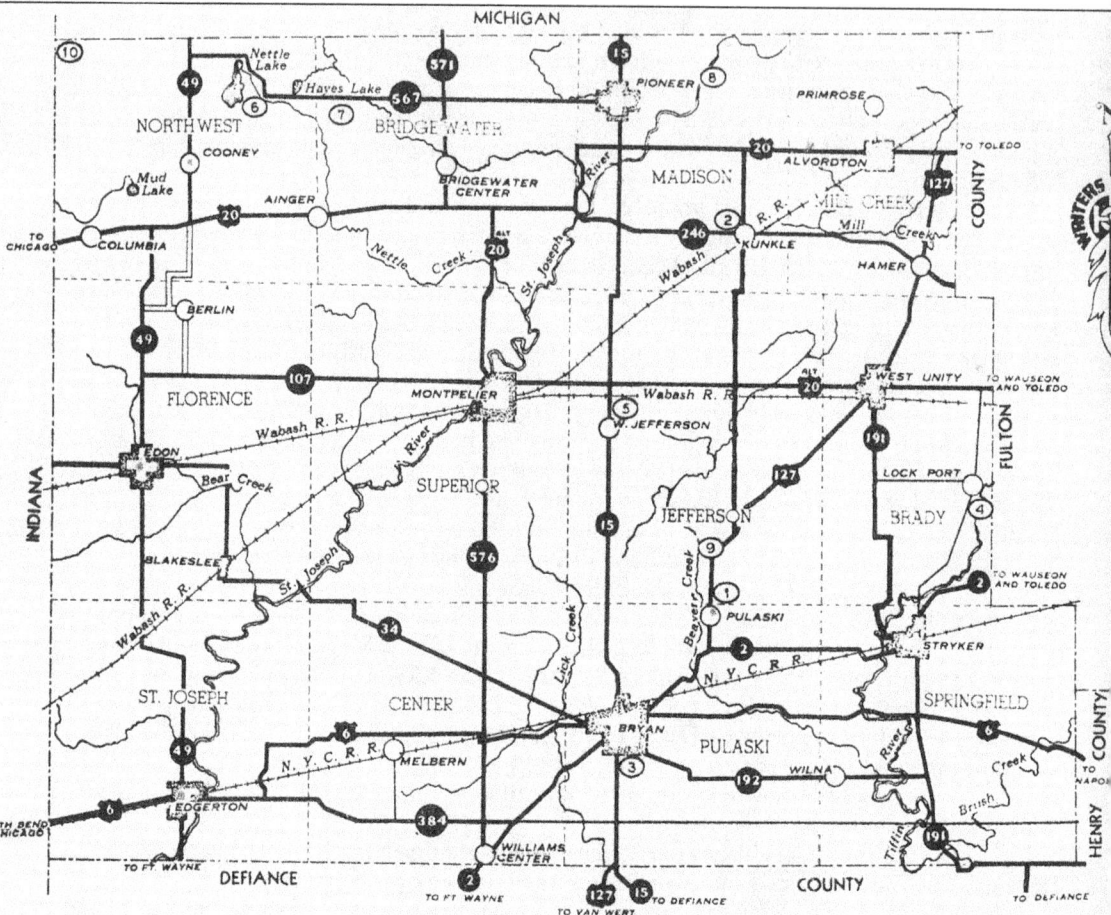

This is a map of Williams County showing Bryan as the county seat. (Map reproduced from WPA, *Bryan and Williams County*.)

One

SETTLING THE
"FOUNTAIN CITY"

The pioneers who settled Bryan were necessarily a hearty lot. Stories—perhaps legends—have been passed down of early settlers killing deer in their yards with a hoe or even their bare hands, and local lore has it that men and boys fished in a pond where the courthouse now stands. Farming was the first and primary occupation, and with the draining of the Great Black Swamp in the 1850s, more and more intrepid folks from "back East" were making their way to Williams County to try their luck at tilling the soil. Clearing the land to make way for farming destroyed much of the natural habitat, and within only a couple of decades the larger game—bear and bobcat—were driven from the area, and wolves were scarcely seen.

Early settlers sometimes had more to fear from each other. In 1847, when a prosperous farmer's five-year-old son went missing the village turned to one Andrew Jackson Tyler, a self-professed psychic who eked out a living by revealing the whereabouts of lost or stray farm animals. When consulted, Tyler prophesied that the boy was dead and would be found "near green leaves, under wood and beside water." Considering the environment of Williams County at the time, it could hardly have been otherwise. Soon, it was revealed that Tyler and his dimwitted accomplice, Daniel Heckerthorn, had kidnapped the child and sought to profit in his discovery. Whether by intent or accident, however, the child had died. The two were arrested and tried for murder, and Tyler's execution—the only known public hanging in Bryan—was carried out downtown.

There were other challenges to the peace, such as the night a horse thief, Sile Doty, rode into town, but hardly any frontier village could have done better. By and large, the first citizens of Bryan were a God-fearing, honest lot, who worked hard, and on occasion, drank hard too. Thanks to photographer John Beach, some images of those days have been captured for posterity. Many of his photographs are presented here, providing evocative snapshots of Bryan's early history.

John A. Bryan (1794–1864), founder of Bryan, Ohio, was a diplomat, politician, newspaper publisher, and land agent. Bryan (left) began his career as a lawyer in Olean, New York, and served as a district attorney and state legislator. He moved to Columbus, Ohio, in 1829 and became a newspaper publisher. In 1833, he was elected state auditor and sold his newspaper business. As a land agent for the American Land Company of New York, he purchased undeveloped land that he sold to settlers in northern Ohio. From 1844 to 1845, he served as the US chargé d'affaires to Peru under Pres. John Tyler. He settled in Wisconsin in 1850 and became the editor of the *Milwaukee Commercial* newspaper. Bryan remained active as a land agent until his death in May 1864. His wife, Eliza, is pictured below.

Agriculture has played a central role in Bryan's economy from the start. Although sharecropping was much more prevalent in the Southern states, especially after the Civil War, it was not uncommon in Northern states such as Ohio. In this photograph, African American sharecroppers are seen tilling soil in a cornfield while a supervisor on horseback looks on. The location and farm are not identified.

In this photograph, taken around the turn of the 20th century, a farmer uses his steam-engine tractor to power a wheat threshing machine. The farm was located on what is now West High Street.

Farming was not the only agricultural activity in the early history of Williams County. Pictured here is a "camp" set up for the collection and processing of maple syrup. Maple trees grew in abundance in northwest Ohio, and the sap provided a form of sweetener for early settlers.

In the mid-1860s, Silas "Sile" Doty, an infamous horse thief, counterfeiter, highwayman, and common criminal known throughout the Midwest, was apprehended in Bryan in a livery stable near the old Yates House hotel on South Walnut Street. He was jailed and handled with extreme caution before being returned to Michigan to serve yet another prison sentence. (Illustration reproduced from WPA, *Bryan and Williams County*.)

One of the more colorful personalities to grace the streets of Bryan in its early days was one Jacob Newman Free, a.k.a. the "Immortal J.N." Born in Mansfield, Ohio, in 1826, Free lived a rather nomadic life and traveled from town to town giving unsolicited advice and long orations on his personal philosophy to anyone who would listen. He was rumored to have struck gold in California in his younger days, though after returning to Ohio, never seemed to have much cash on hand. During the Civil War, he was prone to giving spontaneous public speeches defending the views of both sides and arguing that both were equally right and equally wrong. Although eccentric, his celebrity was such that he was said to have had a free pass to ride the rails and innkeepers welcomed him without charge. He remained dedicated to his own self-avowed mission of "lifting the veil of error for others to see the truth" until being committed to an asylum in Toledo where he died in 1906.

This illustration depicts the Sherwood-Nelson house, one of the first upscale homes built in Bryan. Gen. Isaac R. Sherwood occupied this residence on Portland Street from the 1850s until 1865, followed by John W. Nelson, attorney and banker, and Gustav Christman, co-owner of the Christman Hotel, who resided there until 1956 when the house was razed to make room for the new high school.

Originally built as a hotel in 1844 by John Will, the Yates House, formerly located at the corner of South Walnut and East Butler Streets, was converted into a boardinghouse by John Yates in 1894. This photograph shows the house in early 1946 during an auction, not long before it was razed by Grant Brown to make room for his Brownie's restaurant.

16

The first ostensibly permanent courthouse built on the public square was erected in 1846 and was a considerable improvement over its log predecessor. The photograph above shows the west side of the old courthouse as it appeared in the mid-1860s before the 1875 fire that devastated much of the east side of the square. A brick privy can be seen at center, as indoor plumbing was yet to be installed. The community woodpile is also visible. The photograph below shows the northwest corner of the courthouse in 1887. The quaint white picket fence has been replaced with metal pipes fitted through wood posts, which served as a hitching rail for horses. Although more functional, it was certainly less aesthetically pleasing.

18

This c. 1960s map of Bryan identifies the major streets, parks, highways, and railroads in the city. It is provided to assist in locating the buildings and landmarks shown in the pages that follow.

CARTERS CORNERS 1860

The building at the top center of this photograph, taken in 1860, is Carter's Corners, which occupied the northeast corner of the intersection of High and Main Streets from 1843 to 1899. Built by Dr. Thomas Kent, the structure was originally designed to be a saloon, but it housed numerous other businesses over the years including a drugstore and restaurant. The *Bryan Democrat* newspaper printing office occupied the second floor from 1865 to 1898. Carter's Corners was also a popular hangout for "habitual loafers" who sought shade under the building's old wooden awnings. A fire on May 25, 1899, damaged the building so badly that it had to be razed. It was replaced by the three-story structure occupied by Farmers National Bank and later Citizens National Bank, and more recently, the Williams County Public Library.

This 1860 postcard shows the center and eastern half of the north side of the square on the 100 block of West High Street. The three-story brick building (left) was erected in 1859 and was commonly known as the Union Block. The building to its immediate right covered in posters was the county jail, which was moved from its original location on North Lynn Street to this site in 1848. It was Bryan's second jail and was constructed from the logs and materials of the original jail built in 1842. This structure was briefly home to the infamous Sile Doty after his arrest, and also housed child murderer Andrew Jackson Tyler, who was publicly hanged just east of this site in January 1849. The small building to the right of the jail housed Hook and Ladder Company No. 1, Bryan's first fire department. The bell attached to the roof was used to alert the town of a fire. The remaining structures to the right were grocery stores.

This photograph, also taken in 1860, shows the Union Block and jail (right) on the north side of West High Street looking west beyond the alley that divides the block today. At center is A.A. Allen's General Store, which occupied the Crall building, said to have been the first brick business block in Bryan, built in 1852.

The south side of the 200 block of West High Street is seen here as it appeared in 1860. The second building from the left, advertising oysters, is the Lager Beer Saloon. The house of Joseph Fulton is next to the right, and the three-story wooden structure at center is the Bryan House hotel. In the distance on the right, the spire of the old Baptist church can be seen.

The northern end of the east side of the square is seen above across the lawn of the old courthouse in this photograph from 1860. The white picket fence that once surrounded the courthouse can be seen in the foreground. The three-story brick building at center was known as the Letcher Block, likely because brothers Orlando and William Letcher occupied offices there. They were reported to be cousins of Pres. James A. Garfield. The Letcher building burned in March 1875, taking with it McQuilkin's corner grocery to the left. Two additional three-story brick buildings were erected adjacent to the south side of the Letcher building in 1868 (below), and these survived the 1875 fire and remain standing today.

This photograph shows the southern half of the east side of the square along South Main Street before the Letcher Block (left) was destroyed in the 1875 fire. The two-story brick building housing Ashton's store (right) was built in 1855. The water pump formerly located on the southeast corner of the square is visible to the right.

Pictured here is West Butler Street on the south side of the square in the 1860s. The first structure on the right is Andrew Clonst's Boot, Shoe, and Leather store, which occupied the former site of the first government office building in Bryan. Reportedly a small log hut, it was built in 1841 and later also served as the first schoolhouse.

This late 1860s photograph provides a view of the west side of the 100 block of North Main Street. At center is E.B. Willett's Marble Works, with tombstones clearly visible out front. Willett's remained in business at this location from 1861 to 1916.

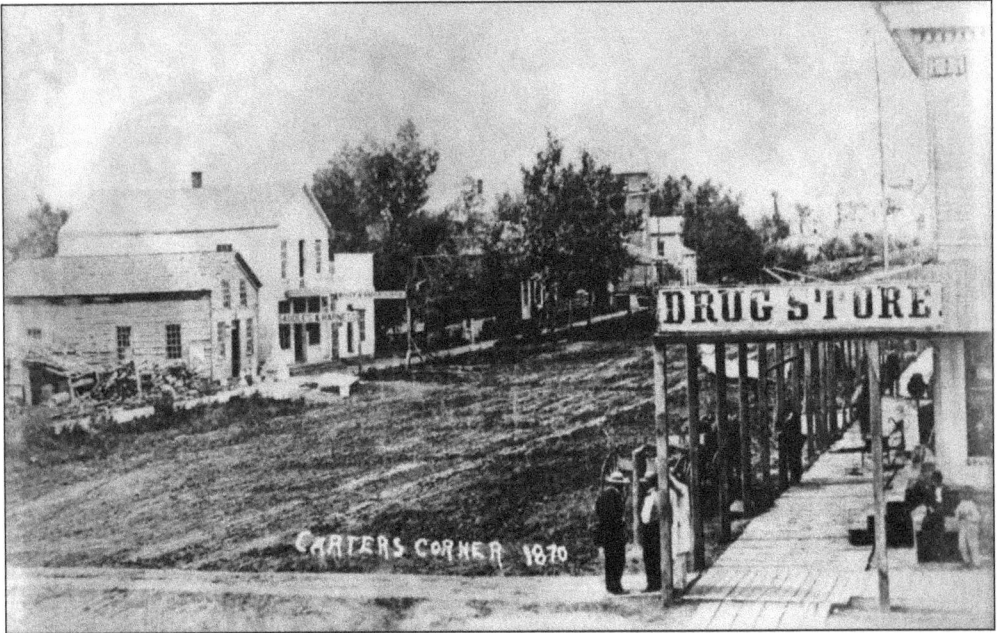

Seen here is the 100 block of North Main Street as it appeared in 1870. The second building from the left was William Harding's Saddles and Harness shop, established in 1867. Across the street and on the right was Carter's Corners drugstore, which then still featured a wooden awning and plank board sidewalk.

Formerly located at 233 North Lynn Street, this building was home to Bryan's first college, the Bryan Normal School, also known as the Mykrantz Academy. Founded by Charles W. Mykrantz in 1867, the college provided education for area teachers, but closed in 1883 when Mykrantz left town. Later, the building served temporarily as a courthouse, a drug and alcohol rehabilitation institution, and finally, a private residence in 1894.

Bryan's water was thought by some to have healing properties. Originally opened as the Park Hotel on South Main Street, the building seen here was converted into the "Mineral Bathhouse," a spa where the infirm could bathe in warm sulfur water heated by a natural gas well tapped in 1888. The building was razed not long after this photograph was taken in 1910.

The Michigan Southern and Northern Indiana Railroad was first to arrive in Bryan with an east-west line to Toledo in 1855. It was briefly the Lake Shore and then became the New York Central after being taken over by Cornelius Vanderbilt in 1869. The passenger depot (above) was built in 1871 on the northernmost edge of town on Front Street, now Paige Street. Passengers had to cross the tracks to board, so in 1886, the depot was moved to the south side of the tracks, together with a new telegraph office. The Cincinnati, Jackson & Mackinaw (CJ&M) Railroad extended its north-south line through Bryan in 1887, providing the town access to two major railroads and thus greatly facilitating the growth of local commerce. The CJ&M depot can be seen below just beyond the water tower.

Schuyler E. Blakeslee, attorney and prominent citizen for whom one of the streets of Bryan and a nearby village were named, is seen here returning to his home on South Lynn Street on the west side of the square. Dave Miller's Boot and Shoe Repair shop is on the left, Shaw's Jewelry Store is center, and Charles Nebelung's barbershop is to the right.

Proper ladies dressed formally when going about in public in the late 19th century. This 1886 photograph, taken on South Lynn Street on the west side of the Courthouse Square, shows from left to right, Lillie Shaw, Sarah Elliot, Carrie Moore, and Jennie Parrott.

Broom brigades became popular across the country in the 1880s. These were organizations of women who dressed in uniforms or costumes of a sort and practiced military-style drills, though instead of carrying firearms they toted brooms. Mark Twain once wrote of a broom brigade performance he observed in New Orleans, stating, "I saw them go through their complex manual with grace, spirit, and admirable precision. I saw them do everything which a human being can possibly do with a broom, except sweep." The members of Bryan's Broom Brigade are, from left to right, (first row) Sgt. Birdie Welker, Allie Walker, Louie Willett, and Cpt. Mamie Relyra; (second row) Bertie Niederaur, Annie Gish, Cora Yunck, Mary Dorshinner, and Addie Patterson; (third row) Anna Willett, Carrie Dales, Mina Boothman, Anne Harper, and Ettie Teeple.

In the winter of 1887, Albert C. Spangler lashed together this train of six bobsleds, pulled by a team of six horses, and gave the children of Bryan a surprise trip around town. The last sled in the train was reserved for the Bryan Cornet Band, which provided music along the way. The photograph was taken looking north on South Lynn Street on the west side of the square.

Bernice and Edgar Connin, children of Alex Connin, are playing on a wooden sidewalk in this 1890s photograph. Wooden sidewalks were still common in Bryan in the late 19th century. The old Mykrantz Academy building on North Lynn Street is visible to the left.

Frank and Jennie (Parrott) Niederaur and their son Phillip stroll home along West High Street after paying a visit to their friends, the Morrisons, in this 1890s photograph. The Hotel Williams, formerly located at the intersection of High and Beech Streets, is visible before them, and the courthouse tower can be seen in the distance beyond to the left.

This stately Victorian-era home on Center Street, pictured here in the late 19th century, was the residence of Theo Kampf, who ran a jewelry store on South Main Street. Kampf is pictured with his wife Bertha and their children, son Ted (left), and daughter Salome (right). The infant in the photograph is unidentified. This house still stands at this location.

Pictured here are the jurists of the George Burchell trial in front of the courthouse in 1892. The Burchell brothers, George and Michael, conspired with Walter Plummer and William Elkins to rob Arthur Brown, a local well driller, who had been seen hitting the town with a large sum of money he had earned for a recently completed job. On May 4, 1892, after a night of heavy drinking, George Burchell lured Brown into an alley downtown where the four men then assaulted and robbed Brown, leaving him to die of his injuries. The Burchell brothers were arrested two days later and held for trial. George Burchell, 25 years old, and younger brother Michael were found guilty of second-degree murder and sentenced to life imprisonment with hard labor. Plummer and Elkins evaded arrest until May 1893, but were also arrested, tried, and found guilty of murder in the second degree.

Two

Bryan Becomes Modern

By the turn of the 20th century, Bryan had become a bustling little boomtown. The arrival of the railroad connecting Bryan to Toledo in 1855 opened the village to new development. With the railroad came the telegraph, and the first telephone was connected in 1879. By 1882, telephones were in general use throughout Williams County. Electricity was more widely available too.

Transportation was also becoming easier. In June 1905, the Toledo and Indiana (T&I) Railway Company built an electric interurban line linking Bryan to Toledo. Powered by a generating plant in Stryker, the T&I could travel up to 65 miles per hour and made the trip to Toledo in just about two hours. A roundtrip ticket cost only $1.55. Automobiles were also increasingly popular, with interest generated by national and international "auto tours" whose cross-country races were designed to promote the new technology. Bryan's old dirt streets were being paved in brick by 1903, and by 1915, some were being paved over with asphalt. New highways, such as Route 6, soon cut through town.

Despite the quickening pace of modernization, however, the people of Bryan remained traditional in many ways. In the early to mid-20th century, Bryan was still known as a center of horse breeding and sales and hosted an annual horse fair that drew visitors from across state lines. The people were known for being stubborn about their politics too. A government study of Bryan from 1941 describes its citizens as being "devotees of politics and horseflesh . . . [and] no other community north of the Ohio River ever demonstrated Bryan's enthusiasm over the ballot box and the stable." A decidedly Democratic populace from the start, Bryan turned staunchly Republican by the 1940s.

The people of Bryan suffered through the Great Depression and the world wars along with the rest of the nation. The Works Progress Administration (WPA) under the New Deal helped to keep the city growing—and the people working—by funding building projects that resulted in a new post office, a new American Legion building, and the Moore Park pool, to name a few. Bryan became a city in 1940 but retained the feel of a small, bucolic Midwestern town.

In 1888, the state legislature of Ohio approved a bill to fund construction of a new courthouse. Demolition of the old courthouse began soon after and the cornerstone of the new building was set on April 30, 1889. The partially constructed courthouse is seen here in 1889.

The west side of the courthouse can be seen in this 1891 photograph looking northeast from beyond the intersection of West Butler and South Lynn Streets. Construction of the courthouse appears to be nearly complete, save for the installation of the clock in the building's signature clock tower.

Pictured here is the 100 block of West High Street as viewed looking north from the courthouse clock tower in the early 20th century. The building immediately left of the alley is the Union Block, and the taller three-story structure to the right is the Long Building, erected in 1869. Today, this side of the square looks much as it did at the time of this photograph.

At the turn of the 20th century, Bryan could be described as a town on the move, in this case literally. In this photograph, an entire store is being relocated by tractor on an oversized trailer. The Hotel Williams at the intersection of West High and South Beech Streets is visible on the right.

Merchants of James A. Elder's Livery and Sale Stable pause along the 100 block of South Lynn Street on the west side of the square in 1901. Behind the team of horses can be seen the Kerr Brothers' General Store, which opened in 1898, and the Blakeslee home to the right.

Located at the intersection of West Butler and South Lynn Streets on the south side of the square, the row of buildings seen here in 1902 was known as the "Centennial Block," ostensibly because it was constructed in 1876, one hundred years after the birth of the United States. These buildings replaced the wooden structures that were destroyed by fire—a suspected case of arson—in 1876.

Members of the Connin and Beach families gather on July 16, 1904, to celebrate the dedication of their street—most likely North Lynn Street near the intersection of West Mulberry Street, where both families lived—as it was about to be paved with red brick. The bricks to be used in paving can be seen lying on both sides of the street.

This c. 1905 photograph, taken from the southeast corner of the square, shows some of the first electric poles erected in downtown Bryan. A private company supplied power to the town starting in 1889, but electricity was not widely available to more rural areas for another 20 years. Also visible are the second bandstand (center) and a trough for watering horses to the right.

The horse and buggy remained the primary means of transportation around the turn of the century, as shown in this photograph taken in 1906 on the southwest corner of the square. Stopping to have their pictures taken are Mrs. John R. Neff (left) and her granddaughter Florence Wilma Neff Roe (right).

This 1909 postcard shows the 100 block of South Main Street on the east side of the square on a very busy Saturday afternoon. Note the wooden sidewalks and hitching posts for horses still surrounding the Courthouse Square. A lone automobile is visible at center left among the crowd of horses and carriages.

This tranquil winter scene from 1909 shows the west side of the 200 block of North Main Street looking north from Bryan Street. The stately brick home at left was owned by Mandana Willett. It was replaced by a gas station in 1921 after being sold to Empire Petroleum.

This photograph, taken from the northeast side of the square looking south and west, shows a bustling downtown street scene in the winter of 1909. Horses and sleighs were the means of transport in the day, and not even heavy snow covering the streets could stop commerce and traffic. The courthouse is visible in the background.

Long-distance automobile races began as early as 1893. In 1908, the New York to Paris Automobile Tour, the most ambitious road race conceived up to that time, made its way through Bryan. Six automobile crews entered the city-to-city race, which had a special twist: contestants first had to travel *west* across the United States. Scheduled stops out of New York included Chicago, San Francisco, Seattle, and Valdez, Alaska. After being shipped to Japan and then to Vladivostok, Russia, the racers trekked across the vast expanse of Siberia to Moscow and on to St. Petersburg, then Berlin, and finally to Paris. One of the six cars entered in the race, the French Motobloc, led by crew chief Baron Charles Godard, is pictured here stopping briefly for a photograph on the south side of the 200 block of West High Street on a snowy February afternoon. The Motobloc later broke down in Iowa and did not finish the race.

Another cross-country race to come through Bryan was the Garford Auto Tour in 1911. Some of the tour's participants are seen here stopped in front of the Christman Hotel on North Main Street. Pictured are two Studebaker-Garford Touring Cars, presumably 1908 models.

Bryan began to see more traffic in the early 20th century with the increase in popularity of the automobile and new highways, such as Route 6, being built through town. Pictured here front and center is the Hupmobile, produced by the Hupp Motor Company from 1909 to 1940. It appears to be a 1924 model touring car.

This photograph shows South Lynn Street on the west side of the square in 1912. This block was once the location of the Masonic Temple (center), as well as some of Bryan's most popular stores and shops, including Gorny-Winzeler's and Carroll-Ames hardware, the latter of which burned in a 1948 fire and relocated to the old Temple Theater on West High Street.

Bryan's high water table and ample water supply were a blessing for thirsty travelers and shoppers alike. Pictured at center right in this 1912 photograph is the canopy-covered public water pump that once graced the northwest corner of the intersection of Main and High Streets. The three-story brick building on the corner stood from 1865 to 1973, and housed the First National Bank, the post office, and a telegraph office.

With snowballs in hand, these two unidentified gentlemen appear ready to create a bit of mischief. This photograph shows the east side of the square looking north along South Main Street. The year is likely 1900, as the charred south side of the Niederaur building is still visible after the fire that decimated Carter's Corners in May 1899, and the Farmers National (later Citizens) Bank has yet to be built.

With very few exceptions, crime has never been a significant problem in Bryan. But projecting an appearance of strong law enforcement has always been a good way to keep the peace. Pictured in this 1912 photograph, and looking quite intimidating, are Sam S. Wineland (left), who served as sheriff from 1912 to 1916, and his deputy, Benner Wineland (right).

43

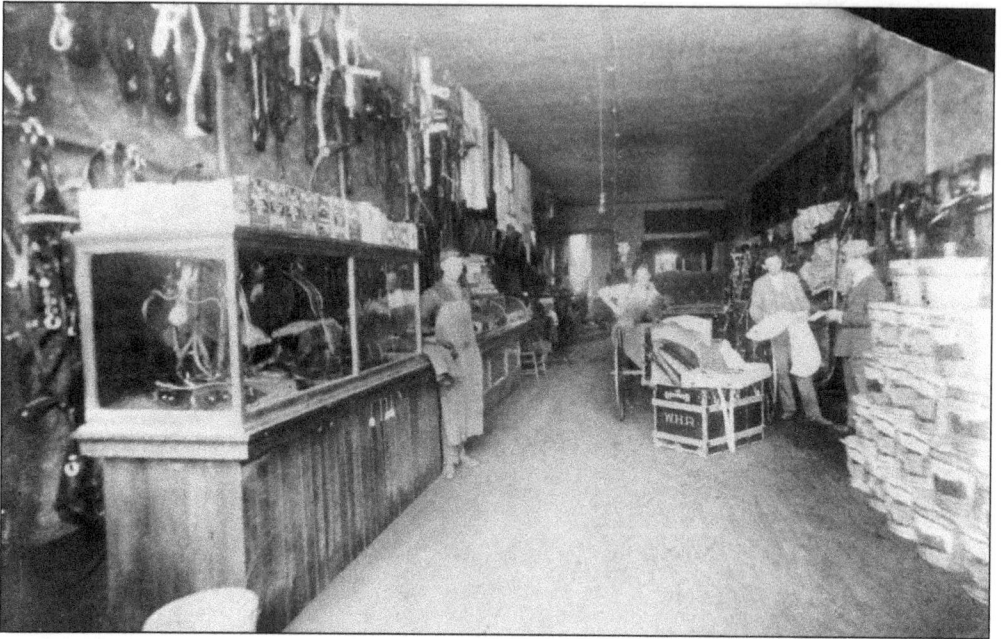

William H. Riley and his son Harold J. Riley operated this harness shop and leather goods dealership on South Main Street on the east side of the square from 1895 to around 1923. Bryan had many such enterprises that thrived in the late 19th century, but most all of them were put out of business with the rise in popularity of the automobile in the early 20th century.

The arrival of the airplane in the skies over Bryan was yet another sign of modernization. Airmail service began in the United States in May 1918, and Bryan was designated as one of two stops in Ohio along the New York to Chicago route. Here, a crowd gathers around a Curtiss JN-4H "Jenny" biplane, the first and most commonly used airplane for mail delivery at that time.

Street sprinklers, such as the one seen here driven by Alex Partee in 1920, were still commonly used in the early 20th century to dampen dirt roads in order to keep the dust down and, largely, to wash away refuse and horse manure from the newer brick roads around town.

Bryan provided a number of municipal services, and horses remained integral to many of those through the 1920s. The team of white horses pictured here, for example, not only pulled the town's fire equipment and street sprinkler, but also hauled gravel for the streets and carried away refuse to the dump, as noted on the "Dump Wagon" driven here, again, by Alex Partee.

Samuel E. Folk (1863–1940), was the son of William Folk, owner and operator of the Ohio Rifle Works and Machine Shop on North Main Street. Samuel was one of the most prominent citizens in Bryan's early history. In his youth he manufactured firearms with his father, then worked for a short time as a locomotive fireman for the Lakeshore and Michigan Southern Railroad. In 1912, he patented an innovative water pump and started the S.E. Folk Company to manufacture it; the factory was located on the present site of the Ohio Art Company on East High Street. Folk also invented an oil-burning stove for home heating and built his own steam-powered automobile. But he was also a dedicated city employee and served as the superintendent of the Bryan Light and Water Works from 1902 until his death in 1940.

This artesian well, one of many that graced the early landscape of Bryan, was drilled on Garden Street to supply the Bryan Municipal Water System. Samuel Folk, superintendant of the Bryan Light and Water Works, is pictured on the left.

The high water table that was once a curse for the first settlers of the area became an advantage once modern technology was applied to the problem. In this photograph dated 1908, drillers tap an artesian well near the Cincinnati Northern Railroad along North Garden Street, one of the many wells that provided an ample supply of clean water for the people of the Fountain City.

The Atlas Diesel Generator pictured here at the Bryan Light and Water Works plant provided significant improvements in electric power production and supply from 1912 to 1919. Posing before the Atlas generator, nicknamed "Big George," are superintendant Samuel E. Folk (left) and George Brown (right), plant engineer.

Employees of the Bryan Electric Light and Water Works are pictured here with the No. 1 Nordberg 1,000 kilowatt generator in 1933. The employees are, from left to right, Al Schatzer, Arthur Caster, Mack Calvin, Dale Crummel, Wallace Parnham, Tiny Algeo, Harley "Shorty" McCafferly, Russell Pickering, and Samuel E. Folk, superintendant.

From 1905 to 1939, the Toledo & Indiana Railway (T&I) operated an electric interurban rail service shuttling passengers roundtrip from Bryan to Toledo. The interurban is seen above pulling into the Bryan terminus, formerly located on the south side of the 100 block of East High Street. In the photograph below, Car No. 135 pauses briefly as it departs the station. The building to the left is the old Episcopal Church, later the site of the Markey Children's Library. Travel by electric rail, much like a trolley car as seen here, was once quite popular in northwest Ohio. But competition from the automobile and new bus services eventually drove the T&I and most other electric rail companies out of business.

Bryan's post office relocated several times: from South Lynn Street (1863), to East High Street (1873), to the First National Bank building on Main and High Streets (1898), and to South Main Street (1919–1935), until settling permanently at 142 North Main Street in 1936, when the WPA provided assistance for the construction of a new federal building. The post office is seen here in 1960, prior to the addition of the south wing in 1962.

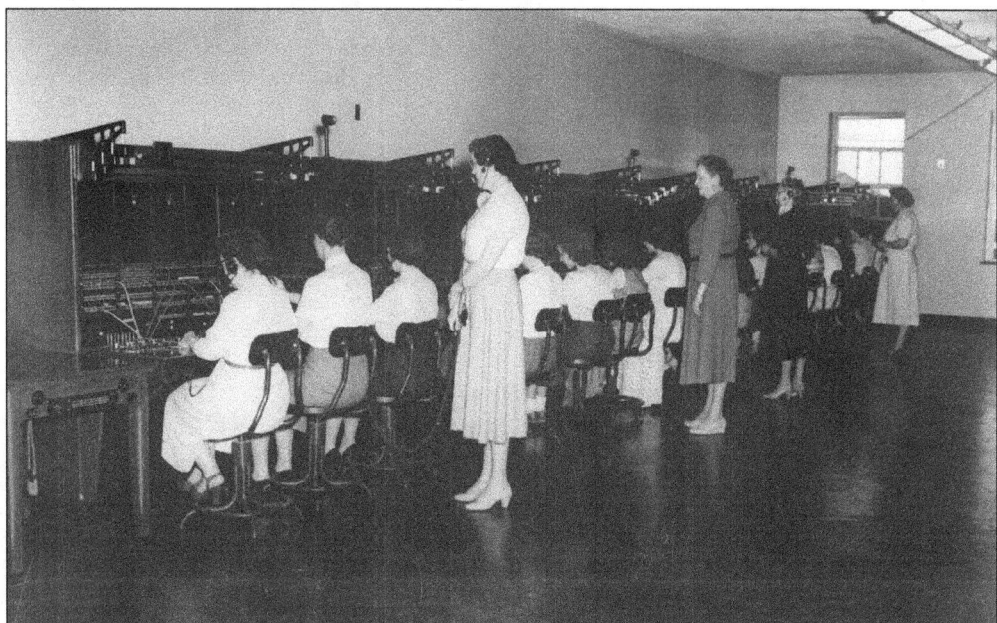

In the early years of the telephone, connections had to be made manually by switchboard operators, one of the few occupations once dominated by women, that is, before automated electronic switching became widespread in the 1960s and rendered the switchboard operator obsolete. This photograph is presumed to be of employees of the Williams County Telephone Company at work in the 1930s. (Photograph courtesy of Eldon Smith.)

The US Census of 1940 determined that the population of Bryan had finally exceeded 5,000, qualifying it as a city. This photograph, taken in 1941, shows the first joint organizational meeting of the Bryan City Council and the Bryan Board of Trustees of Public Affairs convening to draft a charter for the new city government. Pictured from left to right are board members O.L. Kelly, Harrison Miller, Mayor Charles R. Ames (standing), councilmen W.R. Holmes, Ben Hoffman, Vernon E. Allion, Clyde Easterly, and Fred Bowman, and board member Harold D. Kensinger. The round receptacles seen on the floor at each end of the table are cuspidors—more commonly known as "spittoons"—which were still in common use at the time. They soon disappeared from public view, however, as cigarettes came to replace chewing tobacco.

Dedicated on November 25, 1874, this building served as both a city hall and an engine house for the fire department. The first floor housed firefighting equipment, while the second floor served as the firemen's chambers with additional meeting rooms for the city council. City firefighters posed for this formal photograph (above) in 1910, showing off both the old, traditional horse-drawn pumps and the new motorized vehicles that are more modern. The photograph below shows the city hall in 1947. In addition to new garage doors for the firehouse, a wing was added (right) to house the offices of the Bryan Police Department.

Samuel Folk is seen here (center) operating the Bryan Fire Department's new Paterson steam-powered water pump, dubbed "Steamer Number One," at the corner of High and Main Streets. The Paterson steamer was purchased in 1873 and remained in use until 1918, when it was replaced by the Metropolitan.

Pictured here is Percy Connin on the Metropolitan steamer that served as Bryan's second steam-powered water pump from 1918. This rudimentary fire engine was originally designed to be pulled by a two-horse team, but was later modified to be pulled by a truck. It is seen here during a Jubilee parade in the late 1940s and is now on display at the Williams County Historical Museum in Montpelier, Ohio.

Members of the Bryan Volunteer Fire Department in 1948 included, from left to right, (first row) O.H. Rubel, secretary; Percy Connin, captain; Walter McFadden, chief; Bobby Sharrock, mascot; Howard Maneval, assistant chief; Richard Poynter, lieutenant; and Lee Bunting, treasurer; (second row, standing) Richard Eager (son of Guy Eager), Donald Peters, Robert Parrott, Cletus Dreher, Fred Wolff, Chester Steerhoff, Guy "Mike" Eager (driver), Carl Thiel, Hal Spires, and Ed Merillot.

Fire Chief Walter McFadden was one of two chiefs to die in the line of duty up to the 1940s. Shortly after this picture was taken for the Firemen's Convention of 1948, Chief McFadden died responding to a fire at the sawmill and lumberyard on East Edgerton Street.

Firefighters continued to prove their mettle as seen in this photograph from 1948 when fire destroyed stores on the 100 block of South Lynn Street on the west side of the square. The fire was reported to have started in the Carroll-Ames Hardware store (left) and spread to Gorny-Winzeler's (center). Both stores were devastated and forced to relocate.

On April 2, 1951, the Bryan Fire Department responded to a call concerning an overheated tar kettle in a downtown parking lot. When firefighter Guy "Mike" Eager attempted to douse the flame with an extinguishing "bomb," the kettle exploded, engulfing him in flaming tar. Eager survived but sustained injuries that forced his retirement from the department, which he had served for 21 years.

The Williams County Jail—Bryan's third jail—was built in 1869 and is one of the city's oldest remaining buildings. The photograph above shows the jail, located at 218 West Bryan Street, as it appeared in the early 1930s before undergoing extensive renovation by the WPA in 1939. After the renovation, the jail was described as "one of the most modern county penal institutions in the State, adequately equipped to provide sanitary quarters for men, women, and juvenile offenders, and escape-proof cells for desperate inmates." The jail was expanded and further renovations made in 1964, when Bryan Street was still made of red bricks, as can be seen in the photograph below. A covered passage once connected the jail to the old sheriff's residence, the latter being visible on the right.

Officers of the Bryan Police Department pose with their vehicles in 1932. The officers are, from left to right, Sheriff Leroy Siders, Mickey Fletcher, Red Dewees, and Norman Barnes. The officer with the motorcycle is unidentified.

The police tower, the small structure seen in this 1946 photograph, occupied this spot at the northeast corner of the Courthouse Square from 1940 to 1965. It served as a shelter and office for police on location, who likely helped direct traffic at the increasingly busy intersection of High and Main Streets.

Traffic lights, such as the one seen in the middle of the intersection of High and Main Streets in this c. 1947 photograph, were not uncommon in the first half of the 20th century. By the 1950s, however, most had been replaced with the hanging types seen today. The old-style street lamps are also visible here, as is the former First National Bank building on the corner.

Many of the streets of Bryan were once made of red brick. But by 1915, civic leaders had begun to pave over some of the brick streets with asphalt. In this photograph, apparently taken in the 1940s, a steamroller smoothes the surface of West Butler Street as it gets a new pavement.

The courthouse also received some necessary maintenance around this time. In this 1947 photograph, H.E. Throne is seen giving the face of the courthouse clock a new coat of paint. Perched as he was, high above the ground on the courthouse tower, Throne might have reminded those below of the death-defying stunts once performed by the likes of Bryan natives J. Harry Six and Charles "Minor" Leichty (see pages 105 and 107).

More aerial demonstrations of courage were necessary when the Weaver Construction Company replaced the courthouse roof. In this October 1950 photograph, the scaffolding used by the construction crew to reach the dizzying heights on the west side of the courthouse tower can be seen to the left, while the scaffolding around the roof itself appears as an illuminated crown.

In July 1966, the New York Central Railroad flirted with the idea of introducing high-speed rail service and tested the M-497, a modified Budd commuter car fitted with two GE J47-19 jet engines, seen here passing the Aro water tower on the north side of Bryan. Although the M-497 set a light-rail speed record at nearly 184 miles per hour, the idea of providing high-speed commercial rail service was not pursued.

After relocating several times since 1918, the Bryan airport finally found a permanent home. In 1964, Ohio governor James Rhodes declared all counties in the state must have an airport. The Williams County Airport servicing Bryan was then built on the Richard Schreder farm at 16288 County Road D, about two miles east of the city. The main hangar of the airport is pictured here in autumn 1968.

Three

A VIBRANT COMMUNITY

All communities must have good schools, libraries, hospitals, and an efficient municipal infrastructure to function. But it is the people and their dedication to fellow citizens that make a community thrive. Bryan's many churches, fraternal orders, and charitable organizations have contributed much over the years and, in many ways, have shaped the city as it stands today. Bryan has historically been largely a Judeo-Christian community, with most Christian denominations represented. Methodist, Baptist, Lutheran, Presbyterian, and Catholic churches can be found throughout the city. Fraternal associations date back to the founding of the village, with such organizations as the Order of the Eastern Star and the Freemasons establishing an early presence and the Eagles, Lions, Kiwanis, and Moose, to name only a few, founding local chapters more recently.

Bryan's schools have always been at the heart of the community, beginning in 1841 with a humble one-room schoolhouse—a log cabin. Soon, in 1845, a wood-frame building was erected on West Butler Street to accommodate the growing population of children. In 1858, Bryan's first brick schoolhouse, the Butler Street School, was constructed on the same site. Additional schools were built in the 1870s and 1880s, such as the Cherry and Walnut Street schools. In 1885, the Park School was built on South Portland Street to educate high school students exclusively. A college, the Bryan Normal School or "Mykrantz Academy," founded and operated by Charles W. Mykrantz from 1867 to 1874, provided training for local teachers. New high schools were built in 1903, and again in 1956, to provide better facilities for new generations of Golden Bears.

But Bryan has one more special ingredient to make its community unique: the city band. Since 1852, when John Connin formed the first civic band, and through its many incarnations as the Fountain City Band, the Northwestern Silver Cornet Band, the Tubbs Municipal Band, the American Legion Band, the Bryan Civic Band, and the Bryan City Band, it has provided the soundtrack to the city's history. Now the longest enduring city band in the state and one of the oldest in the nation, the Bryan City Band continues to make the community vibrant.

Built in 1858, the Butler Street School was the first brick schoolhouse in Bryan. Also known as the Foundry School and the Bryan Union School, it replaced the town's first wood-frame school, built in 1845, and was erected on the same site. In this photograph, the American flag drapes the school in observance of the death of Pres. Abraham Lincoln on April 15, 1865.

The Cherry Street School was erected in 1874 at the northwest corner of Cherry and Mulberry Streets. Originally intended as a high school, it served as a primary school instead due to increasing enrollment at the grade school level. Some alleged the building was unsafe, and it was razed in 1917 with the opening of the Lincoln Elementary School on East Butler Street.

Built in 1885 on South Portland Street, the Park School, also known as the Central School, served as Bryan's first dedicated high school. The building has been described as resembling a Greek cross, being entirely symmetrical with identical entrances on each side. The building was razed in 1956 to make room for the high school that presently occupies the site.

The Methodist Episcopal Church (left), built in 1895, is pictured at the intersection of West Butler and South Beech Streets shortly after the turn of the century. At center is the Bryan High School, built in 1903, which was later converted for use as a junior high school. Further to the right, looking north on Beech Street, is the Presbyterian Church, also built in 1903.

The Bryan Public Library (above) located at 107 East High Street, is seen as it appeared when built in 1903 with a generous $10,000 endowment from the Carnegie Foundation. The library has since undergone significant renovations and additions. The dome was removed in 1955, and the first major addition was erected in 1957. In 1960, John C. Markey pledged $50,000 in matching funds for a children's library. Over $115,000 was raised by the community, including Markey's donation, resulting in the dedication and opening of the Ruth Edwards Markey Children's Library (below) on May 23, 1963. More branches opened in the following years, and in 1997, the library expanded countywide and was renamed the Williams County Public Library.

On March 30, 1949, the children of Miss Margery Poland's Lincoln Elementary School kindergarten class were keenly focused on the reading of an Easter story during a visit to the Bryan Public Library. The students are, from left to right, (first row) David Randels, Mary Bowers, Lowell Evers, and Barbara Krill; (second row) Kay Posy, Barbara Bard, David Castor, Johnnie Adams, Gwendolyn Hageman, Dorothy Grim, and Mary Ann McNamee; (third row) Patty Hitt, Sandra Levy, Phillip Watson, Patrick O'Neil, and Susan Seigel; (fourth row) Michael Ruble, Kathleen Wolf, Kathy Ball, Bill Isaac, Henry Warvel, Jerra Mae Marshall, Hank Wilde, and Dawn Humbarger. From the start, the library has been committed to engaging imaginations and improving children's literacy. The Markey Children's Library wing (opposite page below) continues to fulfill that mission even today.

Hospitals are an integral part of any community, but Bryan did not have a modern medical facility until the first hospital (above) was founded by Dr. Don F. Cameron in 1936. This photograph shows the southwest side of the original Cameron Hospital building on West High Street. The first hospital had only one operating room, 17 patient beds, and living quarters for the nurses. It was built at a cost of approximately $40,000. The hospital has since undergone several renovations with significant additions greatly enhancing the ability to provide care. The first addition was completed in 1950, and a northeast wing was added in 1958. These additions brought patient capacity up to 62 beds, expanded radiological services, and provided new offices for the physicians. The third addition added a north wing (below), and was completed in 1966.

The fourth major addition to the hospital was completed in 1978 at a cost of approximately $4 million and provided significant upgrades in compliance with state and federal regulations. The new wing (above), greatly expanded hospital services, while the old section (at right) became obstetrics and administrative offices. The name was then changed to Bryan Community Hospital Inc., and the original structure was designated the Cameron Building. In 2008, plans were approved for further renovations expanding the new Bryan Community Hospital and Wellness Center (CHWC) to over 200,000 square feet. The renovated hospital, located at 433 West High Street, is seen below after renovations in 2012. The bright colors of the new facades reflect the heritage of the hospital, with the original Cameron Building highlighted in red (right).

The 1945 photograph to the left shows the monument that once stood in Court Park to honor the soldiers of Williams County who had perished in the Civil War and World War I. The plaque on the monument reads: "In Memory of the Unreturned." The monument below was erected on the northwest corner of the square in the late 1940s in honor of the soldiers, sailors, and marines who had given their lives in World War II. A memorial honoring veterans that was located for many years in the Fountain Grove Cemetery on the south side of the city was relocated to Court Park in 1989.

American Legion Post 284 received its charter in December 1919 and was named in honor of Lt. Charles E. Arnold (right), a Bryan native who perished in World War I at the Battle of the Argonne Forest, France, during the Meuse-Argonne offensive in 1918. The Legion post formerly occupied several locations around town, including rooms above the Grand Army of the Republic (GAR) hall on the south side of the square, above Cy Demas's Candy Kitchen shop, and from 1928 to 1934, above the old post office, before the building pictured below at 519 East Butler Street was erected in 1936 with the financial assistance of the WPA. Pictured raising the flag are Bryan veterans, from left to right, Gerald Smith, Cy Traush, Howard Hurd, Tom Fleming, John Goll, Richard Sanders, and Eldon Smith.

The Boy Scouts of America was founded in 1910 and established a strong presence in Williams County and Bryan not long after. Pictured here is the Color Guard of Explorer Post 16 in 1960. From left to right are (first row, kneeling) Gregory Van Gundy and Don Galliers; (second row) Army Reserve sergeant Sam Shook (advisor), Neil Wertz, David Waters, Lawrence Bigler, Theodore Kunkle, and unidentified.

The Bryan Area Foundation, established in 1969, is a charitable nonprofit organization founded to serve as "a leader, catalyst and resource for charitable giving." In 1995, the foundation's charter members, pictured here, were honored for 25 years of service. They are, from left to right, (first row) Dr. H.R. Mayberry, Richard Reed, and Grant Brown; (second row) Bill Weaver, Randolph Bard, Wayne Shaffer, George Isaac Jr., Bruce Benedict, Ford Cullis, and Ted Spangler.

Pictured here is the original St. Patrick's Church on the northeast corner of Walnut and Trevitt Streets. The church and parochial school, now located on South Portland Street, were built in 1959 and are affiliated with the Catholic Diocese of Toledo.

This 1907 photograph shows the interior of the Methodist Episcopal Church, located on the corner of West Butler and South Beech Streets. Built in 1895, the church is one of the oldest still standing in the city. In its early days it was known for having one of the grandest pipe organs in the area.

John Connin (1829–1915) is often credited as being the founder of the city band. He had 15 children by two wives and may be considered the progenitor and grand patriarch of the Connin family, which was prominent in the early history of Bryan. He formed Bryan's first known band in 1852 and in so doing, started a long-lasting Bryan institution.

The Northwestern Silver Cornet Band dated back to the Civil War and nearly folded when several members were mustered into the 48th Union Regimental Band. Fortunately, a few were able to remain behind and kept the organization going. They are pictured here in 1876, a decade after the war. Henry Wertz, director, is first on the left in the second row.

One of the many incarnations of the city band, the Tubbs Municipal Band, is seen here in 1910. "Professor" Forrest A. Tubbs (first row second from left), arrived in Bryan in 1892 and served as band director until he passed in 1926. He is credited with starting Bryan's first high school orchestra and integrating music education into the school curriculum.

The continuity and longevity of the city band tradition owed much to the Connin family. This 1928 photograph of the Bryan Civic Band shows Dale Connin (front row, center), who served as director from 1926 to 1962. His father Alex (back row, fifth from left), was also a long-time band member, as were others members of the Connin family throughout the years

The bandstand has long been a focal point of the Courthouse Square. The brick bandstand pictured here was built in 1935 and replaced the old wooden structures that once occupied the northeast and southeast corners of the park. It stood for 60 years, until replaced by a new, larger bandstand in 1998. The Bryan City Band is pictured here giving a performance in the early 1960s.

John Hartman served as supervisor of music and band director for Bryan City Schools from 1943 to 1973, with his wife, Pauline Virginia "Fritzi" Hartman, serving as substitute in 1944–1945 while he was on active duty in the US Navy during World War II. Hartman also served as director of the Bryan City Band for nearly 50 years and gave his last performance in July 2009.

From its beginning in 1852, the city band played at just about every public celebration or occasion that warranted music. But over the years, new technologies such as the radio and tape recordings threatened to replace the band at public functions, and the city band found itself performing on fewer occasions. By the early 1980s, however, the Bryan City Band (or Bryan Civic Band) could claim the title of oldest and longest continuing city band in the state and one of the oldest in the nation. Under the direction of John Hartman (second row, first on left), the band played summertime concerts on the square every Wednesday evening, now a long-standing Bryan tradition. Where once the band was on hand to provide music for an event, today the band's performance is an event unto itself. Pictured here are members of the city band in 1980. Since World War II, the band has been comprised of both teachers and students, as well as other musically talented members of the Bryan community.

These four gentlemen comprised a singing group called the Crescent Quartette. They were all Bryan businessmen who followed their passion for singing on the side. The group performed at the Republican National Convention in St. Louis in 1896. Pictured are, from left to right, E.E. Newman, I.E. Gardner, C.S. Roe, and W.W. Morrison.

In the 1950s, Bryan's two musical power couples combined to form the Stump Jumpers, a lighthearted comedy act providing a bit of vaudevillian entertainment for local audiences. The group is seen here during a performance in 1954. They are, from left to right, Orville "Cy" Dally, "Fritzi" Hartman, June Dally, and John Hartman. Bryan teachers Walter and Mabel Robrock, not pictured, were also occasional performers with the troupe.

The Bryan Auditorium is seen here shortly after being built as an addition to the high school on Butler Street in 1917. The original white cement sidewalks and ornamental lantern that once graced the entrance facing High Street have since been removed, but the building itself remains today and still serves as a public auditorium.

The auditorium has hosted numerous concerts by the Bryan High School band, choir, orchestra, and various school and community drama and theater performances. Pictured here are local thespians posing for a publicity still from the 1940s. From left to right are Ed Bowen, Dorothy Oberlin, Charles Coss, Waunetta Scott, Clark Aumend, Mrs. Cass Cullis, Mrs. Grant Brown, Beryl Barber, and Park Doughten.

Mabel Robrock (1910–2001) was a fixture of the Bryan community for decades. She graduated from Hiram College in 1932 with a major in English and a minor in music. She taught in northeast Ohio for several years before moving to Williams County, where she began her distinguished career as a teacher at the former Park School in the 1930s. She later moved on to the new high school where she taught English, French, music, and photography. She served as faculty advisor of the BHS yearbook, the *Zeta Cordia*, and also served as school librarian until her retirement in 1973. After that, she owned and managed The Book Country bookstore for about 20 years before retiring for a second time. In 1995, the Bryan Chamber of Commerce bestowed upon her the Athena Award in recognition of the many ways in which she advanced the cause of women.

Four

COMMERCE AND INDUSTRY

Anyone familiar with Bryan knows the names—Bard, Isaac, Markey, Spangler, and Winzeler—to list only a few. These were the entrepreneurial families who built the city's industries. Some were first generation immigrants, such as George Isaac Sr., who came from Syria at the turn of the century to join family and friends in Ohio. Isaac started from very humble origins selling linens out of a suitcase door to door. In 1906, he started the Isaac Corporation, a small scrap business that later diversified into tire manufacturing (Isaac Tire, 1926), and in 1945, became a Goodyear distributor. In 1906, Arthur Spangler purchased the Gold Leaf Baking Powder Company in Defiance and moved it to Bryan. By 1920, his Spangler Candy Company was on its way to becoming one of the most famous confectioners in the country. Similarly, in 1912, Henry S. Winzeler moved his fledgling Ohio Art Company (1908) to a newly built factory in Bryan and soon diversified from manufacturing metal picture frames into making toys.

Many more profitable enterprises were established around this time, including the Van Camp Packing Company (1908), the Bryan Handle Company (1910), the Holabird Company (1910), Bryan Plumbing and Heating (Bard Manufacturing, 1914), the Paul B. Elder Company (Elder Pharmaceutical, 1929), the Bryan Canning Company (1930), and the Aro Corporation (1930). The post–World War II era saw further growth, and Bryan welcomed Vistron (1951), L.E. Smith (1951), Hayes-Albion Fifty Division (1952), RKO Bottlers (1953), JBM Tool & Die (1955), Bryan Metals (1956), Challenge-Cook Brothers (1957), Allied Moulded Products (1958), Anderson & Vreeland (1961), Bryan Die Cast Products (1964), General Tire & Rubber Company (1967), Emenee Industries (1968), and Tomco Plastics (1970).

Not all of these companies remain today; some have changed ownership and names, and some have gone out of business. But these were some of the industrial enterprises that prospered early on and employed many of the dedicated and hard-working people of Bryan.

This illustration shows the Model Mills steam-powered flour mill, formerly located at the corner of South Beech and Center Streets. Originally built in 1866 by Dallas S. Cowhick and Cyrus Bowman, after changing ownership several times, it was eventually purchased by Philip and Gustav Christman, who changed the name to Bryan City Mills. The mill was abandoned around 1900 in favor of a new mill and elevator north of town.

CHRISTMAN MILL & ELEVATOR,

Formerly located at the intersection of North Walnut and Edgerton Streets, the Christman Mill and Elevator was one of the first modern mills built in Bryan. Owned and operated by the Christman family, the structure burned in 1920. Lewis Christman is seen here atop the elevator next to the flag.

In 1873, Jacob Halm Sr., a German immigrant, built Halm's Fountain City Brewery at the intersection of Beech and Center Streets, replacing a much smaller facility at the site he had purchased from Henry Arnold in 1865. Halm's skill in brewing, coupled with Bryan's ample supply of clear water, resulted in a high-quality beer that quickly became popular with the locals and made Halm's one of the biggest brewers in the area. By 1881, Halm's was selling over 200 barrels per week. Halm met a tragic fate, however, when his coat sleeve caught in a cogwheel and he was pulled into a machine and killed during a factory inspection on March 7, 1883. His son took over the business and was by all accounts doing well until the county voted to go dry in 1908, thus putting an end to one of Bryan's first successful enterprises. Here, father and son pose before the brewery.

Blacksmith Alex Mattox is seen here in front of his wagon repair shop on East Wilson Street in this photograph taken to commemorate the opening of his business in 1874. The large, round window at the center of the structure was taken from the old courthouse upon its demolition.

These dapper men were photographed in front of the Merchant Tailor shop of Herman Wolff, who operated a clothing store in the 100 block of West High Street from 1895. It is uncertain, but likely, that he was a son of David A. Wolff, also known as "Old Reliable," who opened one of Bryan's first tailor shops in 1866.

Located at 128 West High Street in the western half of the old Union Block, Essi's began as a grocer, later became a confectioner, and then was an ice cream parlor. Pictured here in front of their store around the turn of the 20th century are Ferris Essie (left) and Joe Essie (right).

The Dewees family ran this meat market at 128 North Main Street in the building erected by Amos Dewees in 1901. The unidentified gentlemen pictured here presumably include Amos (center) and his son Harry (left).

THE VAN CAMP PACKING CO'S. MILK CONDENSORY, BRYAN O.

The Van Camp Packing Company established a milk condensory plant in 1908 on the north side of East High Street, adjacent to the New York Central Railroad, and began production in March the following year. By 1916, the facility had 30 employees and expanded to include two, two-story brick buildings. For the time, the facility was touted as "the most modern, best-equipped milk evaporating plant in the United States." The Pet Milk Company bought the facility in July 1944 and expanded into can manufacturing in 1947. Declining sales, however, led Pet to discontinue production in 1983. In 1985, the factory was sold to the Quigley Company, which manufactured specialized products for the steel industry. In 1992, the facility was subsequently purchased by Minteq International Inc., a manufacturer of engineered refractory lining systems.

A local branch of the American Express Company operated out of an office on West Butler Street from the late 1800s to about 1930. Competition from the US Postal Service, the telegraph, and later the telephone, however, led the parent company to diversify into finance while local offices such as this closed. An unidentified driver pauses here momentarily to have his photograph taken in 1908.

Despite the many merchant shops flourishing in downtown Bryan after the turn of the century, itinerant peddlers could still be seen in the streets of Bryan and in the surrounding towns and villages. Pictured here is James Daniels, a driver for Frank Malcolm's Cooney Store, around 1915. Such wagons not only made deliveries, but were ideal for providing on-the-spot sales as well.

Although Bryan could claim many fine inns and hotels throughout its early history, few could match the elegance and reputation of the Christman. Built in 1895 on the west side of North Main Street, construction was barely completed when then governor and soon to be president William McKinley and his wife, Ida Saxton, arrived for a brief stay in July. The hotel is seen here on a postcard around 1922.

Cecil Gray, who operated a barbershop in the posh Christman Hotel in the 1920s, points to two empty spaces where shaving mugs from his prized collection should have been. An unknown thief apparently absconded with them in the middle of the night. The collection is now on display at the Williams County Historical Museum in Montpelier, Ohio, sans the missing mugs.

The Blakeslee House, pictured here in the 1930s, was built in 1844 by W.A. Stevens and occupied in that year by attorney Schuyler E. Blakeslee, who used the house as law office and home until his death in 1894. Around that time, Melvin M. Boothman, the first native-born citizen of Williams County to be elected to congress, purchased the house and used it as his law office until he passed in 1904, at which time the practice and building were taken over by his junior partner, Chauncey L. Newcomer. Newcomer and his legal associates occupied the building until 1939, when the house was relocated to 530 South Cherry Street to make room for the Bryan Theater. Pictured here from left to right are (first row) Ruth Peugot, Pat Maneval, LaMoyle Masters, and Dorothy Fetzer; (second row) Gibson L. Fenton, Chauncey L. Newcomer, and Frederick R. Parker.

Built in 1914 and formerly located on the south side of the 100 block of East High Street, this unique structure once housed Huffman's Motor Service and Gleason's restaurant. Ford Greek purchased the building in 1941 and operated an automobile salesroom, service station, and the Palace Bowling Alley upstairs, until 1971. The building was razed in 1973 and replaced with a municipal parking lot.

The Dining Car restaurant pictured here (center left) around 1950 occupied this spot on the 100 block of North Main from 1926 to 1955. The diner's unique facade and convenient location downtown just doors away from the Christman Hotel (right), then Bryan's premier lodging facility, made it a popular local eatery.

Grant Brown capitalized on the emerging postwar automobile culture in 1946 and opened Brownie's Drive-In, one of northwest Ohio's first drive-up restaurants. It is pictured here just after opening for business and before the auto service lot was finished. The restaurant occupied the former site of the Yates House at the corner of South Walnut and East Butler Streets.

This iconic, 1950s-style diner with its signature neon coffee cup sign has been a familiar Bryan landmark since opening in 1965. Founder Lester Bammesberger opened similar restaurants in Florida and Arizona, one of which allegedly served as the inspiration for Mel's Diner on the television sitcom Alice in the 1970s. Lester's closed in 2011 and was sold to a local restaurant chain. (Photograph courtesy of Eldon Smith.)

The Temple Theater (above) opened in 1921 at the site of the old Armory Hall on the northeast corner of West High and Beech Streets. Originally built as a drill hall in 1878 by the veterans of Company E of the 16th Regiment, Ohio National Guard, the building also came to be used for public meetings, dances, and high school graduations. After a fire severely damaged the structure, the veterans sold the building, and ownership changed many times thereafter. It was the home of the Jones Opera House, the Aros Theater, and then the Temple Theater. Carroll-Ames Hardware bought and occupied the building in 1955, relocating again after the disastrous fire that destroyed their original business on South Lynn Street in 1948. The hardware store is seen below in the 1960s.

The Bryan Theater was built in 1940 at 140 South Lynn Street on the former site of the Blakeslee House. Seen here not long after opening, the theater was managed for much of its history by Albert W. Yahraus. The theater underwent extensive renovation in the 1980s when it was converted from a single-screen to a multi-screen theater.

Nothing epitomized the rise of the postwar automobile culture quite like the drive-in theater. Bryan's Hub drive-in opened in May 1950 on the eastern outskirts of the city and at its peak could accommodate about 400 cars. The lone building on the lot housed the projection booth and a concession stand. The Hub closed in 1985. (Photograph courtesy of Richard Cooley.)

Originally organized as the Bryan Businessmen's Association, the Bryan chamber of commerce was incorporated in 1947 and established offices in this building at 138 South Lynn Street in 1957. In 1988, the chamber amended its name and mission statement. Now known as the Bryan Area Chamber of Commerce, its purpose is "to promote Bryan and enhance the quality of life and economic stability of the community."

Chamber of commerce executive officers served voluntarily until 1968, when Albert "Al" Yahraus became the first executive director to receive compensation. Pictured here are Bryan chamber of commerce executive officers, from left to right, Elvin Witzerman, Dr. Fred Richardson, Albert Yahraus, and Tom Herman.

The J.J. Newberry's Store was a classic five and dime started by John Josiah Newberry in Stroudsburg, Pennsylvania, in 1911. By the 1960s, the Newberry family enterprise had expanded to include a chain of over 500 stores throughout the country. The Bryan store, pictured here after extensive renovation in 1961, was a premier local shopping destination until eclipsed by area shopping malls in the 1970s and 1980s.

The newly renovated interior of Newberry's is seen here in October 1961. The variety of merchandise for sale shows continuity from the days of the old general store when most anything could be purchased or ordered. The lunch counter at right is evocative of those found in more upscale department stores from previous decades.

The Aro Equipment Corporation, founded by John C. Markey in 1930, was one of Bryan's first major manufacturers. It originally produced lubricating equipment for automobiles and later expanded into the manufacture of valves, cylinders, and air system components. Ingersoll-Rand purchased Aro in 1990 and folded it into its fluid products division. Pictured here is the Aro plant as it appeared in 1983.

Founded by Dale Bard in 1914, Bard Manufacturing began as a modest heating and plumbing contract business, but by the 1930s was a major producer of oil furnaces. By the 1960s Bard had expanded into air-conditioning and became an industry leader with innovations in wall-mounted heating and cooling units. Bard remains a family-owned enterprise and is one of the largest industrial employers in Bryan.

Chamber of commerce officers and local business executives pose together in this photograph for the groundbreaking ceremony of the General Tire plant in 1966. From left to right are Roger Shook, two unidentified, John Dwyer, Albert Yahraus, Tom Herman, John Marquis, George Isaac Jr., and James Tuttle.

General Tire opened this factory in Bryan in 1967 to manufacture giant tires. In 1987, Continental AG, a German firm, purchased the factory to produce off-road tires. Titan Tire then bought the facility in 2006. Pictured here is the plant at 927 South Union Street as it appeared in 1983.

Founded by Henry S. Winzeler in 1908, the Ohio Art Company began as a small manufacturer of metal picture frames and novelty items in Archbold, Ohio. Winzeler moved production to the Bryan plant (above) in 1912 and diversified into metal lithography. Over 50 million sets of the Cupid Awake/Cupid Asleep frame series (below) were sold, making it Ohio Art's first signature product. The company began to manufacture metal toys from 1917 and soon became popular for its line of tea sets and toy drums. Although it produced several popular toys over the years, including Spudsie the Hot Potato Game and the Bizzy Buzz-Buzz pen, by the 1960s, Ohio Art was best known for its most famous product, the Etch-A-Sketch. (Photographs courtesy of the Ohio Art Company.)

In 1977, Howard W. Winzeler sold his family's controlling shares to then president William Casley (W.C.) Killgallon. In 1978, Killgallon was elected chairman of the board, and his son William Carpenter Killgallon became president and chief executive officer. This photograph memorializes the stock transfer. From left to right are Howard W. Winzeler, William C. Killgallon, W.C. Killgallon, and Howard W. "Chip" Winzeler II. (Photograph courtesy of the Ohio Art Company.)

First conceived by French electrician Andre Cassagnes as a rudimentary drawing toy called the Telecran, in the late 1950s, Jerry Burger, then chief engineer of the Ohio Art Company, modified the design to produce the now familiar classic screen with two knobs. The first Etch-A-Sketch was produced on July 12, 1960, and it has been an icon of American popular culture ever since. (Photograph courtesy of the Ohio Art Company.)

In 1906, Arthur Spangler (pictured) purchased the Gold Leaf Baking Powder Company for $450 at a Defiance County sheriff's sale and moved the company to Bryan. In its earliest years, the company produced baking powder, laundry starch, baking soda, cornstarch, spices, and flavoring. The name of the firm was changed to Spangler Candy Company in 1920, as candy replaced all other items formerly manufactured. (Photograph and caption courtesy of the Spangler Candy Company.)

This photograph was taken in 1908 at the Huenefeld Building, the site of Spangler's second location in downtown Bryan, when the confectioner was called the Spangler Manufacturing Company. Pictured here at the storefront from left to right are Ernest Spangler, Ely Munson, Florence Heign, Carmen Salisbury, Ray Cline, Will Cline, and Arthur Spangler.

The Spangler Candy Company moved to its current location at 400 North Portland Street in 1913. The original building was purchased for $3,100 and measured 110 feet in length. Since that time, the plant has undergone 87 different expansions, and the facility now measures over 525,000 square feet. (Photograph and caption courtesy of the Spangler Candy Company.)

Dum Dums entered the product line in 1953 when Spangler Candy Company purchased the brand from Akron Candy Company where the lollipops originated in 1924. Spangler Candy Company currently makes 10 million Dum Dums each day, averaging about 2.3 billion per year. (Photograph and caption courtesy of the Spangler Candy Company.)

The distinctive three-story brick building above occupied the former site of Carter's Corners at the intersection of High and Main Streets from 1900 to 1962. Over the years, the building housed the *Bryan Democrat* newspaper and numerous other businesses. From 1901 to 1916, the third floor served as a National Guard armory and later was used as a public dance hall. The primary occupant was the Farmers National Bank, which purchased the building in 1901 and remained there until 1933, when it was taken over by the Citizens National Bank. The third floor was removed in 1962 during a major renovation (below), with further remodeling in 1974–1975 leaving the building much as it appears today. Citizens National closed in 1987, and the Williams County Public Library acquired the building in 2006. It is now the WCPL Local History Center.

When it opened in 1963, this branch of the First National Bank, formerly located at 310 South Main Street, was the very first drive-through bank in Bryan and in all of Williams County. The larger structure on the left was added in 1968 and served as First National's new banking center, then touted as the "most up-to-date banking facilities" in Bryan.

Pictured here are members of the board of trustees of the First National Bank in 1978. All were prominent citizens and businessmen in the area. They are, from left to right, Howard W. Winzeler, Henry Ford, Russ Kessen, Fritz Parker, Dave Francisco, Bob Lowe, and Stan Pepple.

Bryan mayor William Runkle, flanked by area merchants, is on hand to cut the unique ribbon made of 28 ten-dollar bills to commemorate the grand opening of the Home Savings and Loan Association branch office at 221 North Main Street in 1982. The bills were subsequently donated to the Bryan United Way. From left to right are Howard Skiles, county commissioner; Woody Woolwine, chamber vice president; Tim Schaefer, Retail Merchants president; Richard Scheele, president; Dorence Arps, chairman of the board of the Home Savings and Loan Association; state senator Ben Baeth; Mayor William Runkle; Mark Rhodes, assistant manager; Paul Allison, manager of the Bryan branch; Kevin McDonald of McDonald construction; Richard Pastor of Pastor and Beilharz architectural firm; Marice Bretthauer, county commissioner; and Robert L. Johnson, chamber executive secretary.

Five

CITY CELEBRATIONS

From early in its history, Bryan has celebrated national holidays and historical events with parades, carnivals, and festive gatherings. Annual horse shows became a summer tradition, as did the homecoming parades. Today, the Independence Day parade and Day in the Park, with fireworks display, cap off a weeklong celebration of fun on the square with the annual jubilee.

Among the most memorable of Independence Day celebrations was that of 1919, held in honor of World War I veterans. On that occasion, fireworks were to be launched from the courthouse tower overlooking Park Square. The first two rockets were fired without a hitch, but the third was defective and exploded prematurely, setting off the remaining 100 fireworks in the tower. Fortunately, the pyrotechnical crew suffered only minor injuries, and the courthouse suffered no permanent damage, but fireworks displays were held elsewhere ever after.

In 1940, Bryan held a weeklong celebration to commemorate 100 years since its founding. There were reenactments of the pioneer days representing the first settlers and Ohio's indigenous inhabitants, many featured in a costume parade complete with covered wagons and floats of Bryan's many firsts. Over 15,000 were estimated to have attended.

The homecoming parade evolved out of the Horse Show, and was held annually during summers until 1947 when there was a contest to rename the event, and Violet Robinson won $25 for coming up with the name "Bryan Jubilee." The first jubilee was held August 14 to 16, and proceeds of the event were used to purchase the Eaton Farm, which was later developed as the city's Recreation Park. The 1949 jubilee parade was especially unique as it featured 40 giant rubber balloons manufactured by Jean Gros Inc. of Pittsburgh, Pennsylvania, and was reminiscent of a miniature Macy's Thanksgiving parade.

Christmas has been celebrated on the Courthouse Square for nearly 100 years. The first Christmas tree was planted in 1913, the first lights strung in 1930, and in 1933, Christmas music was played from the courthouse tower for the first time. The Courthouse Square remains a central venue for holiday celebrations today.

The July 4, 1908, carnival seen here at the intersection of High and Main Streets was the first such event to be held in Bryan and in all of northwest Ohio. A local newspaper reported that "a considerable sum" had been raised "to induce the purveyors of culture and refinement to pause here for a few days."

This photograph, taken looking west on West High Street along the north side of the square during the 1908 carnival, captures a rare glimpse of Bryan at night in the early 20th century. Despite the carnival being in town, the streets appear to be empty, even though the clock in the foreground shows it is only 8:20 p.m.

A major attraction of the 1908 carnival was high diver J. Harry "Daredevil" Six, pictured here diving off a ladder from a height over 100 feet. Six—a Bryan native—was a national celebrity, holding many diving records and billed as the "World's Greatest Headforemost High Diver." He has been credited with being "the first person to put Bryan on the map."

Aerial acrobatics were also a featured attraction of the carnival in 1947. Here, an acrobat—probably one of the Freeland Sisters, a popular troupe at the time—performs death-defying feats high above Park Square. The clock tower of the courthouse is a prominent backdrop to the performance.

THE AIRSHIP, AT THE HOMECOMING, BRYAN O

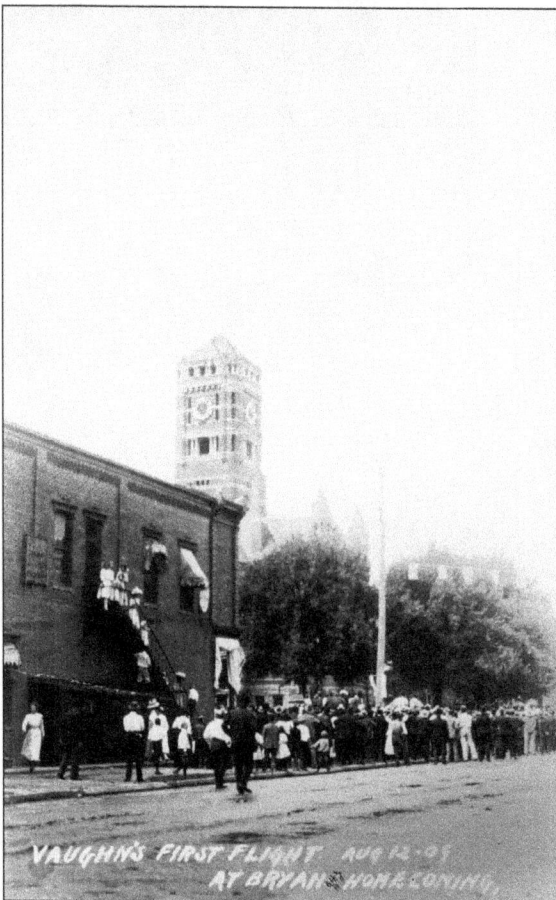

VAUGHN'S FIRST FLIGHT AUG 12-09
AT BRYAN HOMECOMING,

Among the many spectacles to behold throughout Bryan's history was the fly-over of the airship *Stroebel* during the homecoming festival on August 12, 1909. The relative size of the *Stroebel* can be seen above as the pilot, Stanley Vaughn, prepares for takeoff at the intersection of Main and Butler Streets on the southeast corner of the square. Vaughn was allegedly hired by civic leaders and town merchants to help gin up interest in the annual homecoming festivities and gave many Bryan residents their first encounter with manned flight. The *Stroebel* did not disappoint, and those who turned out to witness the event no doubt looked on in amazement as the airship hovered over the majestic courthouse tower (left).

One of the more curious fads to catch on in the 1920s was flagpole sitting. Charles Ray "Minor" Leichty is seen here resting comfortably 180 feet in the air fixed to the flagpole on top of the Williams County Courthouse in Bryan during his world record–setting attempt, which lasted from August 20 to September 10, 1927. Leichty sat for 21 days, one hour, and four minutes. Thousands of spectators turned out to witness the event, even drawing tourists from across the country. Leichty's record was soon broken by Alvin "Shipwreck" Kelly, who started the craze in New York City and reclaimed his title as world record holder. Leichty retired from flagpole sitting and took a job as a window washer. He died on December 4, 1942, falling three stories to the sidewalk while washing the windows of the old Carroll-Ames building, ironically, just across the street from where he had set the world record. The other man in the photograph (below) is C.C. "Dutch" Garber, setting up a radio.

In September 1937, a convoy of US Army trucks (above) brought a company of soldiers to Bryan from Fort Hayes in Columbus to participate in the Northwest Territory Pageant commemorating the 150th anniversary of the Ordinance of 1787, which eventually opened Ohio and much of the upper Midwest to settlement. The soldiers staged a reenactment of a battle against Native Americans for an audience in Park Stadium. The soldiers (below) are, from left to right, Clark Aumend, Bob DeGraff, Grant Brown, and James Lowe.

The Horse Show was a summer event held annually until subsumed by the jubilee in the late 1940s. Pictured here are four entrants in the 1939 Horse Show with their owners, from left to right, Louden H. Eschhofen and sons Rex, Lavon, and Buddy.

Although the county fair was removed to Montpelier in 1886, it continued to be a big draw for the people of Bryan, and horses remained central to the festivities. Harness racing was one of the main attractions of the fair. In this photograph taken in 1939 at the county fairgrounds race track, an unidentified jockey drives his horse around the north turn into the home stretch.

The centennial of the founding of Bryan was celebrated in 1940 with parades, reenactments, and a variety of festivities focusing on the city's 100-year history. The occupants of the covered wagon above represent John Perkins, called "the first white settler of Bryan," and his pioneering family, during the parade held on August 16, 1940. The date 1832 seen on the wagon was the year that the Perkins family allegedly settled in Bryan. In the photograph below, citizens of Bryan dress up in a variety of costumes representing folks imagined to have inhabited the area 100 years prior.

The "train" pictured here was the centerpiece of the jubilee parade of August 13, 1949, which boasted a mile of rubber figures manufactured by Jean Gros Inc. The train was made of 4,000 yards of rubber cloth, 1,000 gallons of rubber paint, 18 miles of rubber tape, and nearly four tons of steel for carriages and wheels and reportedly took eight months to construct.

Bryan area businesses sponsored exhibits in the "Manufacturers & Merchants Display" tent seen here (right) during the jubilee parade of 1949 to draw the crowd's attention to their wares. The parade and jubilee were popular events at the time, and provided local merchants a welcome opportunity to advertise to a large crowd.

A staple feature of most any parade in Bryan for many years was Bud Widmer's Rube Band, seen here being led by Widmer himself marching with baton in a jubilee parade in the late 1940s. Members of the band traveled extensively throughout Ohio to entertain audiences during the summer season. The Rube Band parted ways in the 1970s.

High school marching bands have also been a staple of homecoming and jubilee parades, and high school bands from all over Williams County have participated. The Bryan High School Marching Band, led by director John Hartman, is seen in this photograph from a jubilee parade in the late 1940s.

Another common feature of the jubilee parade was the merchant sponsored float, such as the one seen here advertising the Bryan Manufacturing Company in the late 1940s. Even then, it was not unusual for parade floats to feature beautiful young ladies clad in swimwear, which remains an effective advertising strategy.

This photograph, likely taken during the same parade, shows a float featuring the Honor Guard of the Bryan chapter of the Veterans of Foreign Wars, Post 2489. Extolling patriotism and honoring veterans have long been central themes of the jubilee parade, especially since the parades began to be held on or around the Fourth of July in the 1950s.

One of the highlights of the jubilee was the coronation of the parade queen. On August 14, 1947, Barbara Walker (center) was crowned the first queen of the Bryan Jubilee Parade Pageant. Her attendants and runners-up were Lenore David and Lila Hoffman, pictured here with the queen's flower girls.

In 1962, the Miss "Top of Ohio" Pageant subsumed the Jubilee Queen competition. Contestants for the first pageant with UNCC golf pro Shorty Stockman (center) are, from left to right, Mary Ellen Partee, Gwen M. Jones, Sally Ann Stuller, Karen Kay Woodard, Mary Judith Beck, Sue Tallman, Barbara Roebrock, Margaret Louise Burns, Nancy Moore, and Nancy Ann Thomas. Karen Kay Woodard was declared the winner.

The Bryan High School varsity basketball team won the Northwest Ohio Athletic League (NWOAL) championship tournament in 1958. The managers and coaches (kneeling, first row) are, from left to right, Mike Gray, Mike Whitney, coach Dudley Ebersole, coach Ray Sumpter, and Jerry Myers. The players (standing, second row) are, from left to right, Dariel Young, John White, Ron Miller, John Mignery, Dick Burns, Dave Roebuck, Wayne Long, Lonnie Franks, and Duane Brown.

The Bryan High School championship football team of 1930 went undefeated and untied, a record that remains unbeaten. Pictured here are surviving team members being honored at the old Park Stadium 50 years later in September 1980. They are, from left to right, Paul McKarns, Arthur Kerr, William Gardner, Richard Hathaway, Russell McKarns, Arthur Miller, Charles Weaver, Henry Wonsetler, and Russell Allison.

ABSENT WHEN PICTURE WAS TAKEN: AL HAINES

CULLER

Davidson

The Bryan High School varsity baseball team won the state AA championship in 1975. The team included, from left to right (first row) Brian Blakely, Dave Batt, Doug Grant, Dave McCord, Steve Fireovid, Randy Thorp, Terry Crow, Rick Saneda, and Jeff Grant; (second row) team assistants and managers Marsha Armanini, Tami Force, Karen Snyder, coach Ray Sumpter, Jenny Burns, Shelly Waid, Andrea Benedict, and Jim Tucker; (third row) Chris Saneda, Todd Brewer, Jeff Smith, Rick Gibson, Mark Peugot, Bill Peggs, Ron Miller, Gene Andres, Doug Freed, and unidentified; (fourth row) coach Larry Taylor, coach Doug Parks, BHS principal Joseph Newell, district school superintendant Dr. Dale King, assistant principal Doug Johnson, and coach John Grafton. Absent from the photograph were team members Al Haines and Chuck Culler.

117

The annual Christmas parade marked the official beginning of the holiday season. The arrival of Santa Claus, seen in 1965, was the high point of the parade for children of all ages. Even the old police tower (left) at the northeast corner of the square was decorated in anticipation of the event.

The beautiful lights illuminating the square have long been a featured attraction of the holiday season. More popular among the children, however, was a visit to Santa's workshop (left), which was set up annually on the bandstand just for the holidays. This photograph shows the southwest corner of the square as it appeared in the 1960s.

Six

NOTEWORTHY NATIVES

Bryan is the birthplace and hometown of many gifted individuals who have enjoyed successful careers in a variety of fields. Bryan High School can be particularly proud of its alumni. Those recently achieving national recognition include Mark Winegardner (born 1961), MFA, George Mason University (1985), Burroway Professor of English at Florida State University, and author of *The Godfather Returns* (2004) and *The Godfather's Revenge* (2006), which carry forward the exploits of Mario Puzo's Corleone family from *The Godfather*; Walter J. Koch (born 1962), PhD, University of Cincinnati College of Medicine (1990), professor of pharmacology at the Temple University School of Medicine and director of the Center for Translational Medicine; Marian Goodell (born 1963), MFA, Academy of Art University (1994), co-owner and director of business and communications for the Burning Man experience since 1996; and Jeffrey Masten (born 1964), PhD, University of Pennsylvania (1991), associate professor of English and gender studies, Northwestern University, author of *Textual Intercourse: Collaboration, Authorship, and Sexualities in Renaissance Drama* (1997).

Bryan athletes have also excelled in professional sports, including Frederick "Tom" T. Letcher (1868–?), outfielder for the Milwaukee Brewers (1891); John Herby Himes (1878–1949), outfielder for the St. Louis Cardinals (1905–1906); Robert "Speed" Kelly (1884–1949), third baseman for the Washington Senators (1909); Russell "Russ" Young (1902–1984), NFL fullback for the Dayton Triangles (1925) and catcher for the Milwaukee Brewers (1923–1940) and St. Louis Browns (1931); Bruce Berenyi (born 1954), starting pitcher for the Cincinnati Reds (1980–1984) and the New York Mets (1984–1986); Steve Fireovid (born 1957), pitcher for the San Diego Padres (1981); Chris Carpenter (born 1985), relief pitcher for the Chicago Cubs (2011) and the Boston Red Sox (2012); and Matthew Wisler (born 1992), drafted by the San Diego Padres (2011). In the National Football League, Dave Herman (born 1941), was an offensive lineman for the New York Jets (1964–1973), who went on to defeat the Baltimore Colts in Super Bowl III. In auto racing there is Sam Hornish Jr., winner of the Indianapolis 500 in 2006.

Gen. Isaac R. Sherwood (1835–1925) enlisted as a private in the Union Army in 1861 and by the end of the Civil War, became a brevet brigadier general commanding the 111th Ohio Veteran Volunteer Infantry Regiment. He served two terms as secretary of state, and from 1906, served seven consecutive terms in the US House of Representatives. He was the only member of congress to oppose US entry into World War I. (Photograph courtesy of the Williams County, Ohio Virtual Museum and Andrew Harris.)

Judge John Milton Killits (1858–1938) studied law at George Washington University while serving with the US Signal Bureau in Washington, DC. He served as Williams County prosecutor from 1893 to 1899, then as common pleas court judge from 1905 to 1910. He was appointed to the federal bench in 1910 and presided over several important trials, including a famous libel case concerning the late Pres. Warren G. Harding.

Cullen Yates (1866–1945) was an early 20th-century impressionist landscape painter and member of the National Academy of Art who was particularly popular in America's northeast. His style has been compared to that of Winslow Homer, and his painting *Rock Bound Coast—Cape Ann* hangs in the National Gallery in Washington, DC.

Henry S. Winzeler (1876–1939), entrepreneur, founded the Ohio Art Company, one of the most popular toy companies in the world. From humble beginnings as a dentist in Archbold, Ohio, Winzeler built several businesses and companies, acquired others (such as Chicago's Holabird Manufacturing in 1916), and diversified into new product lines. He retired from Ohio Art in 1927 and moved to Los Angeles where he continued to develop more businesses.

HARRY SIX, CHAMPION HIGH DIVE ROF THE WORLD
CARNIVAL AT BRYAN. O JULY 08

J. Harry Six (1881–1948), world champion high-diving acrobat, became an international celebrity touring North and South America as the star attraction of the Wright Carnival Company. In 1901, he set a world diving record of 136 feet, and in 1915, claimed the title of world's foremost champion high-diver after plunging 104 feet into a pool of water barely 40 inches deep.

Richard Cramer (1889–1960), actor, began his silent screen career in Hollywood in the late 1920s. Often typecast as a villain in low-budget westerns, he later broke through with his distinctive voice with the advent of "the talkies." Cramer made over 200 films from the 1930s to the 1950s and appeared in films featuring such stars as W.C. Fields and Laurel and Hardy.

William Isaac (born 1943) graduated from The Ohio State University with a juris doctorate in 1969 and afterwards served as vice president and general counsel of First Kentucky National. In 1978, he received a presidential appointment to the Federal Deposit Insurance Corporation (FDIC), and served as FDIC chair from 1981 to 1985. He founded the Secura Group in 1985. Isaac is the author of *Senseless Panic: How Washington Failed America*. (Photograph courtesy of William Isaac.)

Born in Bryan and raised in Woodville, Ohio, Col. Terence "Tom" T. Henricks (born 1952) is a 1974 graduate of the US Air Force Academy. He became a NASA astronaut in 1986 upon completing training at the USAF Test Pilot School. Henricks flew four shuttle missions (1991, 1993, 1995, 1996) and was commander of two. He is the recipient of numerous medals and honors, including the Distinguished Flying Cross. (Photograph courtesy of NASA.)

Stephen J. Fireovid (born 1957), MLB pitcher, became a local hero after leading the BHS baseball team to a state AA championship in 1975. He began his major league career with the San Diego Padres in 1981, and pitched for five MLB teams through 1992. His career was chronicled in *The 26th Man: One Minor League Pitcher's Pursuit of a Dream*, coauthored with Mark Winegardner in 1991. (Photograph courtesy of Stephen Fireovid.)

Born in Bryan and raised in Defiance, Ohio, Sam Hornish Jr. (born 1979) is a three-time Indy Car Series Champion (2001, 2002, 2006), and winner of the 2006 Indianapolis 500. Hornish began racing in the NASCAR Busch Series with the Penske racing team in 2006 and retired from IRL competition in 2007, committing to NASCAR competition exclusively from 2008. (Photograph courtesy of Sam Hornish and Sports Management Network.)

Prof. Margaret "Peggy" Goodell (born 1965) is a professor and director of the Stem Cells and Regenerative Medicine Center at Baylor College of Medicine in Houston, Texas. Goodell received her PhD from Cambridge University in England and underwent postdoctoral training at the Massachusetts Institute of Technology (MIT) and Harvard Medical School. At MIT, she developed a novel method for isolating blood-forming stem cells from the bone marrow of mice, which has become widely used to isolate stem cells from a variety of species and adult tissues, including from cancer stem cells. A faculty member of multiple departments at Baylor College of Medicine since 1997, Goodell also holds the Vivian L. Smith Chair in Regenerative Medicine, and is the recipient of numerous awards, including two DeBakey Awards for Excellence in Research (2004, 2010), the Stohlman Scholar Award (2006), the Edith and Peter O'Donnell Award in Medicine (2011), and the Damashek Prize from the American Society of Hematology (2012). Goodell is president elect of the International Society for Experimental Hematology (2012), has served on the board of the International Society for Stem Cell Research (2005–2008), and is chair of the Stem Cells and Regenerative Medicine committee for the American Society of Hematology. Goodell currently directs a laboratory of about 20 students and postdoctoral fellows. (Courtesy of Margaret Goodell.)

BIBLIOGRAPHY

Allen, Mary. *Vignettes of Bryan: 125 Years, 1840 to 1965*. Bryan, OH: Gorny-Winzeler Inc., 1965.

Bowersox, Charles A. *A Standard History of Williams County Ohio, Volume 1*. Chicago and New York: Lewis Publishing Company, 1920.

Bryan Times

Cooley, Richard L. and Kevin M. Maynard. *A Guide to Williams County's History*. Montpelier, OH: Williams County Historical Society, 1995.

Cooley, Richard L. and Kevin M. Maynard. *Temple of Justice: The Story of Williams County's Courthouses*. Montpelier, OH: Williams County Historical Society, 1992.

Culbertson, William L. *Hometown Band: 150 Years of Music and History in Bryan, Ohio*. Mansfield, OH: Bookmasters Inc., 2003.

Patten, Heath Calvin. *Williams County's First Settlers: Prettyman Settlement Archaeological Project*. Bryan, OH: Faded Banner Publications, 2001.

Pool, Douglas A. *City of Bryan Fire Department: 150 Years of Service and Dedication*. Bryan, OH: 2007.

Van Gundy, Paul. *Stories of the Fountain City, 1840–1900*. Bryan, OH: Bryan Area Foundation, 1975.

Workers of the Writers' Program of the Works Projects Administration in the State of Ohio. *Bryan and Williams County*. Washington, DC: Works Projects Administration, 1941.

ABOUT THE ORGANIZATION

The history presented here is based largely on the photographic collection of the Williams County Public Library Local History Center. As such, it is far from being a comprehensive history of the city and is not intended as such. Rather, it is hoped that this book will serve as one window to the city's past as seen through available sources. No doubt there are significant omissions, but historians can only write what the sources reveal. The Local History Center of the Williams County Public Library, together with the Williams County Historical Society, seek to educate the people of Williams County about their past and to preserve that past for future generations. You can help to preserve history by donating your old photographs and significant artifacts to the Local History Center or the Williams County Historical Society. Corrections to this text are also welcome. The author may be contacted at wgrund@bgsu.edu.

Visit us at
arcadiapublishing.com

www.ingramcontent.com/pod-product-compliance
Lightning Source LLC
Chambersburg PA
CBHW080603110426
42813CB00006B/1395